EARTH SCIENCE

Exploring Space

KATE BOEHM JEROME

PICTURE CREDITS
Cover: NASA; page 1 NASA/Science Photo Library/Photo Researchers, Inc.;
pages 2–3 © Hoa Qui/Index Stock Imagery; pages 4-5, 16, 23, 24-25, 25
(bottom left), 26, 27 NASA; page 6 JPL/TSADO/Tom Stack & Assoc.; pages 7, 15
(top left and right), 24 (bottom left) The Granger Collection; pages 8-9, 10-11,
16-17 art by Stephen R. Wagner; page 11 (left) © Breck P. Kent; page 11 (right)
© 1997 by Jerry Lodriguss; page 11(bottom right) Bob Sacha; page 12, 25
(bottom right) ©Dorling Kindersley; page 13 © Frank Zullo/Photo Researchers
Inc.; page 14 illustration © Robin Brickman based on illustration originally
published in Peterson First Guides: Astronomy ©2000 by Jay M. Pasachoff;
page 15 (bottom center) © Scala/Art Resource, NY; pages 17 (inset), 24 (lower
right) © Bettmann/CORBIS; pages 18-19 © Buzzelli/O'Brine/Tom Stack &
Assoc.; page 19 Chuck Place/PlaceStockPhoto.com; page 20 © 2001 Peter
Menzel/ Robo sapiens; page 21 © 1999 Peter Menzel/Robo sapiens; page 22
(top), illustration by Slim Films; page 22 (bottom center) PhotoDisc, Inc.; pages
28-29 Mark Thiessen; page 30 NASA/JPL.

The School Publishing Division is grateful to NASA for their expert advice. We
especially want to thank Debra Hollebeke and Jeff Bingham at NASA
headquarters in Washington, D.C., for their assistance.

Neither the publisher nor the author shall be liable for any damage that may be
caused or sustained or result from conducting any of the activities in this book
without specifically following instructions, undertaking the activities without
proper supervision, or failing to comply with the cautions contained in the book.

Produced through the worldwide resources of the National Geographic Society,
John M. Fahey, Jr., President and Chief Executive Officer; Gilbert M. Grosvenor,
Chairman of the Board; Nina D. Hoffman, Executive Vice President and
President, Books and Education Publishing Group.

PREPARED BY NATIONAL GEOGRAPHIC SCHOOL PUBLISHING
Ericka Markman, Senior Vice President and President, Children's Books and
Education Publishing Group; Steve Mico, Vice President, Editorial Director;
Barbara Seeber, Editorial Manager; Lynda McMurray, Amy Sarver, Project Editors;
Jim Hiscott, Design Manager; Karen Thompson, Art Director; Kristin Hanneman,
Illustrations Manager; Diana Bourdrez, Anne Whittle, Diana Leskovac, Photo
Editors; Christine Higgins, Photo Coordinator; Matt Wascavage, Manager of
Publishing Services; Sean Philpotts, Production Manager; Jane Ponton,
Production Artist.

Cover photo: Astronaut James S. Voss outside space shuttle Atlantis

MANUFACTURING AND QUALITY MANAGEMENT
Christopher A. Liedel, Chief Financial Officer; Phillip L. Schlosser, Director;
Clifton M. Brown III, Manager.

CONSULTANT/REVIEWER
Dr. Timothy Cooney, Professor of Earth Science and Science Education,
University of Northern Iowa

PROGRAM DEVELOPMENT
Kate Boehm Jerome

BOOK DESIGN
3r1 Group

Published by the National Geographic Society
Washington, D.C. 20036-4688

Product No. 4J41264

ISBN-13: 978-0-7922-8870-1
ISBN-10: 0-7922-8870-X

Printed in Canada

11 10 09 08
10 9 8

Sky watchers use the telescope in the observatory at Midi Peak, France.

Contents

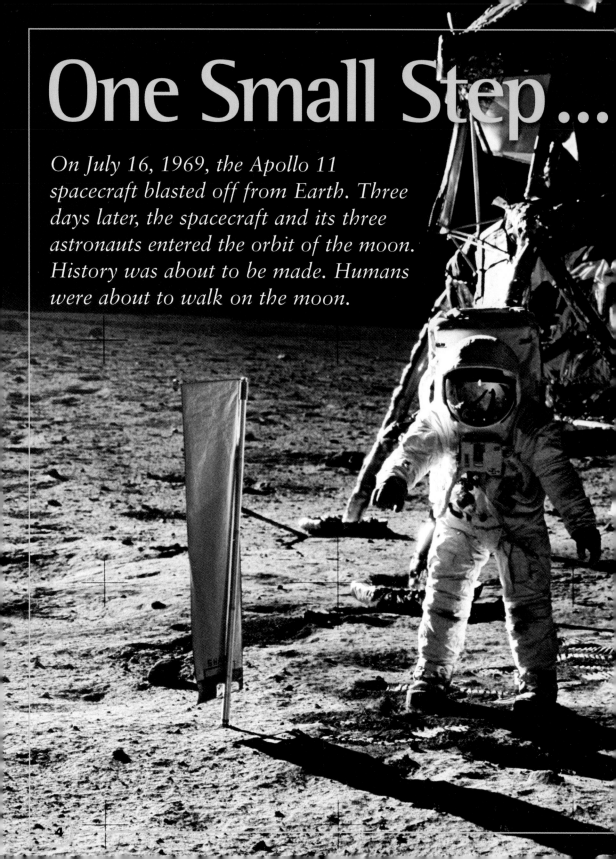

One Small Step...

On July 16, 1969, the Apollo 11 spacecraft blasted off from Earth. Three days later, the spacecraft and its three astronauts entered the orbit of the moon. History was about to be made. Humans were about to walk on the moon.

Astronaut Mike Collins stayed in the command module **orbiting** the moon. Astronauts Neil Armstrong and Edwin "Buzz" Aldrin climbed into a smaller spacecraft to head down to the moon's surface. As the *Eagle* landing craft got closer to the moon, Armstrong spotted trouble. They had missed the ideal landing site. They were headed for a place covered with boulders.

If the *Eagle* were damaged on touchdown, the astronauts could be stuck on the moon forever. They had to act quickly. Armstrong turned off the automatic landing system. He would have to pilot the *Eagle* down himself.

Could the astronauts avoid a crash? Tense moments went by. Instruments showed they had less than 30 seconds worth of fuel left. Then Armstrong's voice crackled over the radio. *"Houston … Tranquillity Base here. The Eagle has landed."* The announcement made the whole world cheer.

The moon landing is just one example of how technology, skill, and imagination come together every day to help us explore our world and beyond. This is a book about where we are now, where we have been, and where we are going. Pay attention now—you just might be one of the brave astronauts flying a spacecraft in the near future!

Edwin Aldrin and the *Eagle*

Chapter 1

The Solar System

Satellites of the Sun

Do you know where you are? Chances are, you can easily name your street, town, state, and country. But what about the position of your planet? Do you know your place in space?

Day after day, year after year, Earth revolves around the sun. The sun is the center of our **solar system** and, in a way, it is our anchor. With the strong pull of its **gravity**, the sun keeps Earth in orbit. The sun also is our major source of energy. Without the sun's light and heat, life on Earth would not exist.

Earth's Neighbors

Earth isn't the only planet that circles the sun. In fact, our solar system is made up of the sun and everything that revolves around it. This includes planets and their moons as well as asteroids, comets, and other objects.

Since ancient times humans have studied the skies. The ancient Greeks made up stories about the stars. Native Americans celebrated the phases of the moon in special ceremonies. Today, advances in technology have improved our understanding of what's out there. We now know, for example, a lot more about the eight planets in our solar system.

Native American sun god mask

What tools do you know about that have helped us learn about our solar system?

The Inner Planets

The four planets closest to the sun are called the inner planets. The inner planets are made up of solid, rocky materials.

Mercury is the planet closest to the sun. Mercury's very thin atmosphere leads to huge changes in temperature. During the day the sun's rays make this planet very hot. At night the thin atmosphere can't keep in heat, and it gets very cold on Mercury.

Venus is next in orbit around the sun. Thick, swirling clouds surround Venus. These clouds trap the sun's energy and make the surface of the planet very hot—more than 450°C (842°F).

Earth's orbit comes next. (Third rock from the sun!) Our planet is largely covered with water. Earth is the only planet in our solar system with enough oxygen in its atmosphere to support life as we know it.

Mars is the fourth inner planet from the sun. Mars is known as the red planet because of its dusty red surface. Scientists think Mars once had a lot of water on it. Some believe there is still ice and even liquid water under its surface.

How do you think the outer planets differ from the inner planets?

THE INNER PLANETS

Mercury   Venus   Earth   Mars   Jupiter

The Outer Planets

The outer planets are farthest from the sun and are much colder than the inner planets. The outer planets are made up mostly of gases, they are also bigger than the inner planets.

Jupiter is the largest of all the planets—more than ten times wider than Earth. Jupiter is mostly gases, but it probably has a solid core. At least 16 moons orbit this huge planet.

Saturn is the sixth planet from the sun. Saturn is famous for the rings of dust and ice that spin around it. People on Earth spotted Saturn's rings back in the 1600s.

At that time telescopes weren't very powerful so it wasn't clear how many rings there were. We now know Saturn has seven major rings.

Uranus also has rings surrounding it. These rings weren't discovered until 1977. When viewed from Earth, Uranus appears to rotate, or spin, on its side.

Neptune is the planet farthest from the sun. It takes Neptune 165 Earth years to orbit the Sun one time. The gases that make up Neptune make it look blue. Like other gas planets, Neptune is a stormy planet with strong winds.

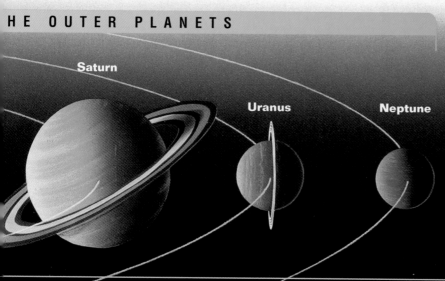

Saturn

Uranus

Neptune

The sun and planets are shown in relative positions. Distance and size are not to scale.

Asteroid belt

Jupiter

Asteroids

Other objects orbit the sun along with big planets and their moons. An **asteroid** is a rock that can be about as small as a house or as large as the state of Texas. Most asteroids revolve around the sun in an asteroid belt located between the orbits of Mars and Jupiter.

Meteoroids

Sometimes small pieces of dust and rock come close enough to Earth to be pulled by gravity into Earth's atmosphere. As the piece of rock or dust, called a **meteoroid**, travels through the air at high speed, it becomes hot and starts to burn. Then it's called a **meteor**. Have you ever seen streaks of light in a clear night sky? These "shooting stars" are meteors.

Although most meteors burn up before they reach the ground, some are large enough so that part of the meteor reaches Earth. If a piece of rock does hit, it's called a **meteorite**. Scientists collect and study meteorites to learn more about where they come from.

Students with a large meteorite

Comet Hale-Bopp

Comets

Often described as "dirty snowballs," **comets** are large chunks of ice, dust, and gas that orbit the sun. Sometimes their orbits take them far away from the sun. When comets get closer to the sun, more of their ice becomes gas. This gas gets pushed out from the comet—so it looks like the comet has a tail. A comet's tail can be millions of kilometers long.

In 1997 the comet Hale-Bopp passed close enough to Earth to be seen. Probably more people saw this comet than any other one in history.

Stay Tuned!

Pluto?

Scientists have decided that Pluto should no longer be called a planet. They say it's too small. In fact, Pluto is smaller than Earth's moon—and it is mostly made of ice like a comet. Pluto has been considered a planet since its discovery in 1930. People now have to get used to one less planet in the solar system.

This boy had his face painted to celebrate the sighting of Halley's comet in 1986. He will be 81 when this famous comet returns.

Eye on the Universe: Gathering Space Data

Scientists have been collecting information about space for hundreds of years. Astonishing discoveries have been made in the last decade with data collected from the Hubble Space Telescope. Collecting vast amounts of data about space, the Hubble is our most powerful eye on the universe.

The Hubble Space Telescope is about as long as a school bus.

Thinking Like a Scientist: Interpreting Data

When scientists **interpret data**, they identify patterns and answer questions with the new information. Scientists have collected data about distances in space. Space is so big that distances are measured in Astronomical Units (AU). One AU is 149.6 million kilometers—the average distance between Earth and the sun. Use the data in the table to answer the questions below.

Planets and Their Orbits

Planet	Average distance from the sun (astronomical units)	Time it takes to orbit the sun (in Earth years)
Mercury	0.4 AU	88 days
Venus	0.7 AU	7.4 months
Earth	1.0 AU	1 year
Mars	1.5 AU	1.9 years
Jupiter	5.2 AU	12 years
Saturn	9.5 AU	29.5 years
Uranus	19.2 AU	84 years
Neptune	30.1 AU	165 years

Which planet takes the longest time to orbit the sun? The shortest time?

What relationship can you see between AU and orbiting times? HINT: Find the distance from the sun to each planet. Then look at the amount of time it takes the planet to orbit the sun.

Chapter 2

Beyond the Solar System

Shooting for the Stars

Have you ever looked at the Big Dipper and Little Dipper in the night sky? If you have, you've looked at the very same stars the ancient Greeks saw thousands of years ago.

The Big Dipper is part of the Ursa Major (Big Bear) constellation. Ursa Minor (Little Bear) is the Little Dipper.

People have always looked to the sky and wondered about what they saw. The ancient Greeks made imaginary connect-the-dot pictures to explain patterns of stars in the sky. Some of these pictures, called **constellations**, were based on stories about the superhuman Greek gods. One myth goes like this.

The Story of Big Bear and Little Bear

The king of the gods, Jupiter, had a wife named Juno. Queen Juno became jealous of a pretty woman named Callisto. One day Queen Juno decided to get rid of Callisto by changing her into a bear.

Callisto was upset. She went home for help. On the way, she ran into her son. He did not recognize her as a bear. He aimed his arrow at her. Just before the arrow flew, Jupiter swept down from the sky and turned Callisto's son into a bear too. Then Jupiter grabbed both bears by the tail and tossed them up into the sky. That's how the Little Bear and Big Bear constellations came to be.

Imaginary stories about constellations may not seem useful to us now. But ancient people had few tools available to them. As technology advanced, so did our understanding of our solar system.

Galileo Galilei: Father of Modern Science

In the early 1600s, an Italian scientist named Galileo Galilei used a telescope to study objects in the sky. Galileo used a simple telescope that allowed him to see things at magnifications 20 times greater than with the naked eye. This may not seem very powerful today, but the telescope allowed Galileo to describe great things. He saw that the moon had craters. He saw that the planet Venus goes through phases just like our moon. He also saw four moons circling Jupiter.

Galileo's discoveries caused him many problems. At the time he lived, people believed that Earth—not the sun—was the center of the solar system. When Galileo interpreted his new data, he began to think differently. He realized that the sun was the center of the solar system. Religious leaders disagreed with this way of thinking. They told him to stop discussing the idea. Galileo chose to give in to the authorities to save his life. But the evidence was there for anyone to see. Eventually, people realized Galileo was right. The sun is the center of our solar system.

How did Galileo's interpretation of data change how people thought about the universe?

Galileo's drawings of our moon

Galileo used this small, handheld telescope to study the universe.

Taking Flight

As centuries of discoveries flew by, it became obvious that humans would not be content to just gaze at the solar system. We wanted to blast off into it as well.

Once again, technology allowed us to accomplish our goal. On October 4, 1957, a Soviet rocket boosted the first human-made **satellite** into space. It was called *Sputnik*, the Russian word for "traveler." Even though Sputnik was nothing more than a small aluminum ball with a radio inside, it started a whole new era of space exploration.

In May 1961 President John F. Kennedy challenged American scientists to land a person on the moon before the end of the 1960s. Scientists faced many obstacles in the quest to do this. For example, to get a spaceship all the way to the moon and back would take a lot of power. Could a rocket engine be built that was powerful enough to make the trip?

President Kennedy

The Big Boost

Rocket engines work because of a basic law of **physics** that says that for every action, there is an equal reaction in the opposite direction. When rocket fuel burns, hot gases are produced. The gases expand rapidly in all directions, but the rocket engine only allows them to escape toward the ground (the action). Because the gases expanding upward can't escape, they push the rocket toward space (the reaction).

Scientists realized that it would be difficult for one heavy rocket loaded with fuel to reach the moon. Instead, they decided to use a multistage rocket. When the fuel in one stage of a multistage rocket is used up, that stage falls away. This makes the rocket lighter, and the engine of the next stage can ignite and thrust the rocket even faster and higher.

Saturn V Multistage Rocket

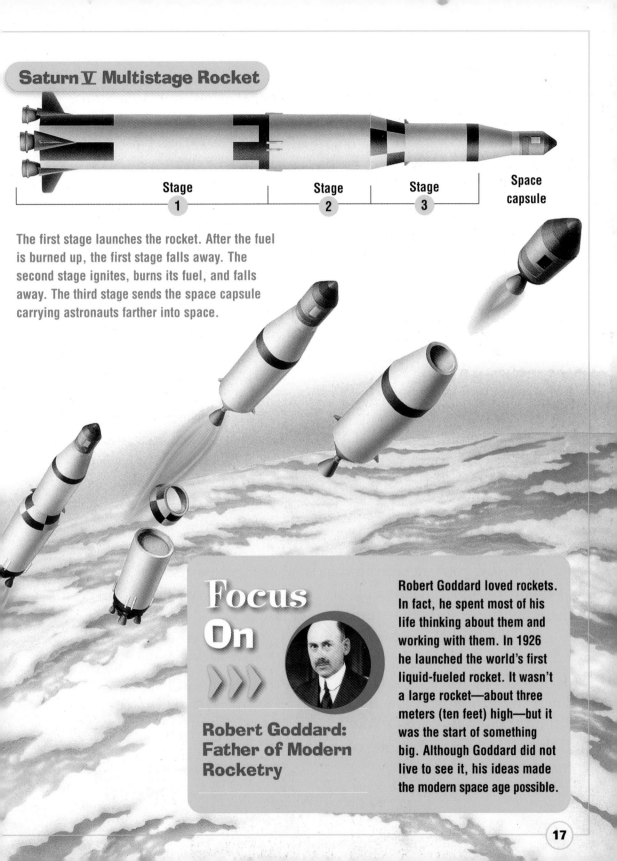

Stage 1 Stage 2 Stage 3 Space capsule

The first stage launches the rocket. After the fuel is burned up, the first stage falls away. The second stage ignites, burns its fuel, and falls away. The third stage sends the space capsule carrying astronauts farther into space.

Focus On

>>>

Robert Goddard: Father of Modern Rocketry

Robert Goddard loved rockets. In fact, he spent most of his life thinking about them and working with them. In 1926 he launched the world's first liquid-fueled rocket. It wasn't a large rocket—about three meters (ten feet) high—but it was the start of something big. Although Goddard did not live to see it, his ideas made the modern space age possible.

17

Mission Accomplished

As you know, Americans successfully landed on the moon in July 1969. Our knowledge of the solar system has increased dramatically since then.

Is there more beyond our solar system? You bet! As you look into the night sky, you can see thousands of points of lights. Almost all of these lights are stars that form a huge system called a **galaxy.** Our solar system makes up a very tiny part of the Milky Way Galaxy. There are probably a few hundred billion stars in the Milky Way Galaxy. Our sun is just one of those stars.

Is there even more beyond our Milky Way Galaxy? Yes, again! There are billions of galaxies in the universe. The distances between these galaxies are great. In fact, light traveling to us from the nearest galaxy similar to the Milky Way has traveled for two million years by the time we see it on Earth!

Word Power

The word *galaxy* comes from the Greek word *gala*, meaning "milk." Our galaxy is known as the Milky Way.

Did you ever

wonder...

... what star is nearest Earth?

The sun is our closest star. However, it takes more than 8 minutes for light, traveling at 300,000 kilometers (186,000 miles) per second, to travel from our "close" star to Earth.

Chapter 3

Life in Space

Space Today and Tomorrow

A tiny piece of space garbage slams into the space station. Alarms sound. A small hole has been punched in an outer panel. Repairs must be made quickly. But how?

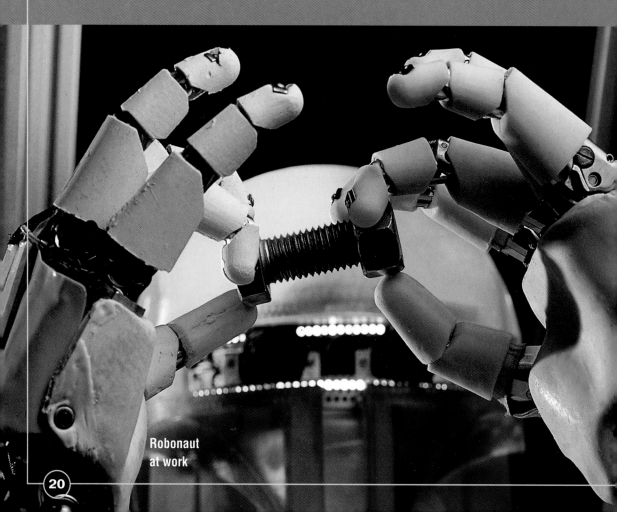

Robonaut at work

Within minutes, a set of eyes is peering at the damage. A Robonaut has arrived to patch the hole. Slowly and carefully the Robonaut's mechanical hands begin to work. Soon the repair is made and the space station is as good as new. The Robonaut waits for the next emergency.

This is not a scene from *Star Wars* or *Star Trek*. The Robonaut is a space robot created to help the astronauts living in the **International Space Station**. It's dangerous for humans to be outside the walls of the space station. But this robot can stand the harsh environment. When the robot is needed, an astronaut inside the space station will control the Robonaut by using **virtual-reality** gloves and headgear.

Modern technology from the space program has changed the way we live on Earth. Today we know not only a lot more about space but also a lot more about Earth. And there is still more to find out!

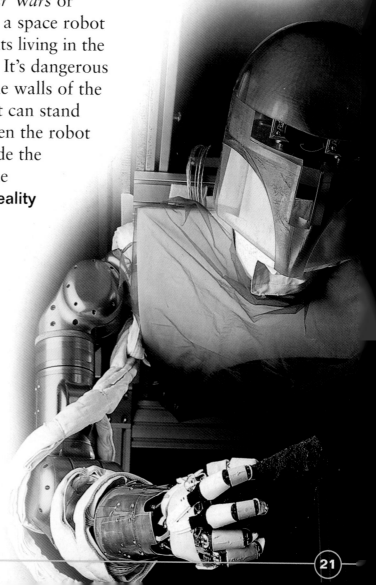

NASA's Robonaut has cameras for eyes, a sturdy body, flexible arms, and hands complete with five fingers.

Sky Watch

Did you know there are more than 2,000 artificial satellites orbiting Earth right now? When you turn on your TV, you are actually tuning in to information from space. The signals don't come from other planets though. A television station on Earth broadcasts a program and **communications satellites** pick up the signals and beam them all over the world.

Communications satellite

Weather satellites help us track weather. They take pictures of the clouds over Earth. Meteorologists study these pictures and give us early warnings of storms and other weather events.

Together Toward the Future

So where do we go from here? One of the most exciting space explorations of all time is happening right now. The International Space Station (ISS) is a joint project that involves 16 countries. It will take some 40 space flights more than 5 years to deliver the parts for assembling the

Interesting Questions ...

Space Age Spin-Offs

Satellites in space provide information we use every day. But many products we use right here on Earth were first developed for the space program and are called spin-offs.

Q: Hey, I don't wear a space suit. What can I possibly use from the space program?

A: Look up. Do you see a smoke detector? Originally, a smoke detector was designed to alert astronauts of smoke or fire in the spacecraft.

Q: OK ... but have they made anything fun?

A: Well, NASA recently worked with a toy company to make a foam glider that's easy to fly. They used ideas from big wind tunnels to design the toy's wings and tail.

entire station. But even before the station is completely finished, international crews of astronauts will live and work there for several months at a time.

The parts of the space station are built here on Earth. Then they are delivered to Earth's orbit by either U.S. space shuttles or Russian rockets. A really important section, or module, was delivered in February 2001. The space shuttle *Atlantis* took up a 16-ton science laboratory named *Destiny*. This incredible module is the first permanent space lab ever.

What are some of the things we hope to learn from studies on the space station? There are many things we need to know. One important question is how long-term space travel might affect the human body. Right now astronauts

Astronaut Ellen Ochoa plays the flute in the weightless environment of space.

lose some bone tissue every time they stay in space. Scientists want to figure out a way to keep this from happening in a weightless environment. This information could be very important some day if we are going to take long trips to Mars and beyond. The adventure has just begun!

Would you like to live on the space station? How would your life be different from your life on Earth?

Word Power

The word *astronaut* comes from two Greek words—*astron*, meaning "star," and *nautes*, meaning "sailor." An astronaut is a person trained to pilot a spacecraft or to conduct experiments in space.

International Space Station

Destiny lab module

Dock for space shuttle

Space Exploration

600 B.C.	1609	1903	1926	1957
Ancient Greeks begin recording constellations.	Galileo uses a telescope to study the universe.	The Wright brothers fly the first successful airplane.	Goddard launches the first liquid-fueled rocket.	The Soviet Union launches Sputnik 1 satellite.

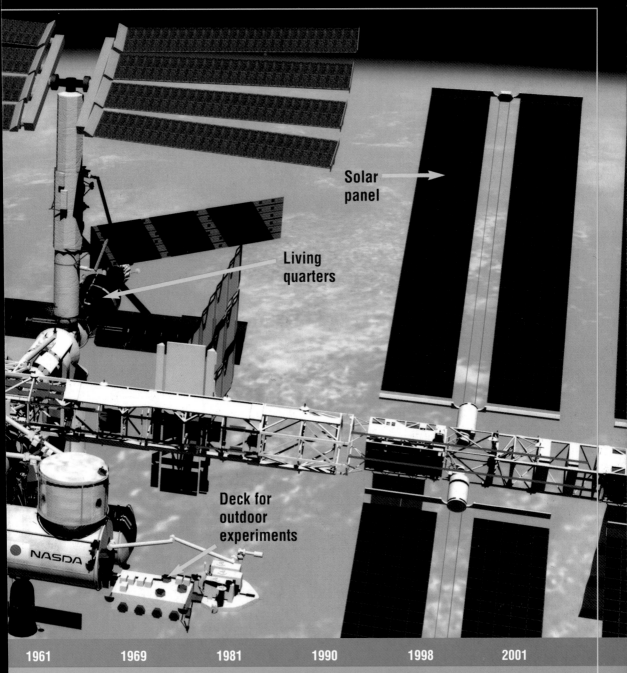

Solar panel

Living quarters

Deck for outdoor experiments

NASDA

1961	1969	1981	1990	1998	2001
Kennedy challenges American scientists to land a person on the moon within the decade.	Apollo 11 mission lands the first person on the moon.	The first space shuttle is launched.	Hubble Space Telescope is deployed.	Construction of the International Space Station (ISS) begins.	ISS receives permanent space lab *Destiny*.

Interpreting Data

We collect lots of new information every day. But the real challenge comes in making sense of it all. One of the skills that helps us understand our observations is called interpreting data. Arranging information in charts, graphs, and tables makes it easier to see patterns and answer questions.

This helps us interpret, or figure out, what the data mean.

The bar graph below shows information about four moons of Jupiter. These moons are called the Galilean satellites. They are named after Galileo Galilei, who first discovered them in 1610.

The Galilean Satellites: Average Distance From Jupiter

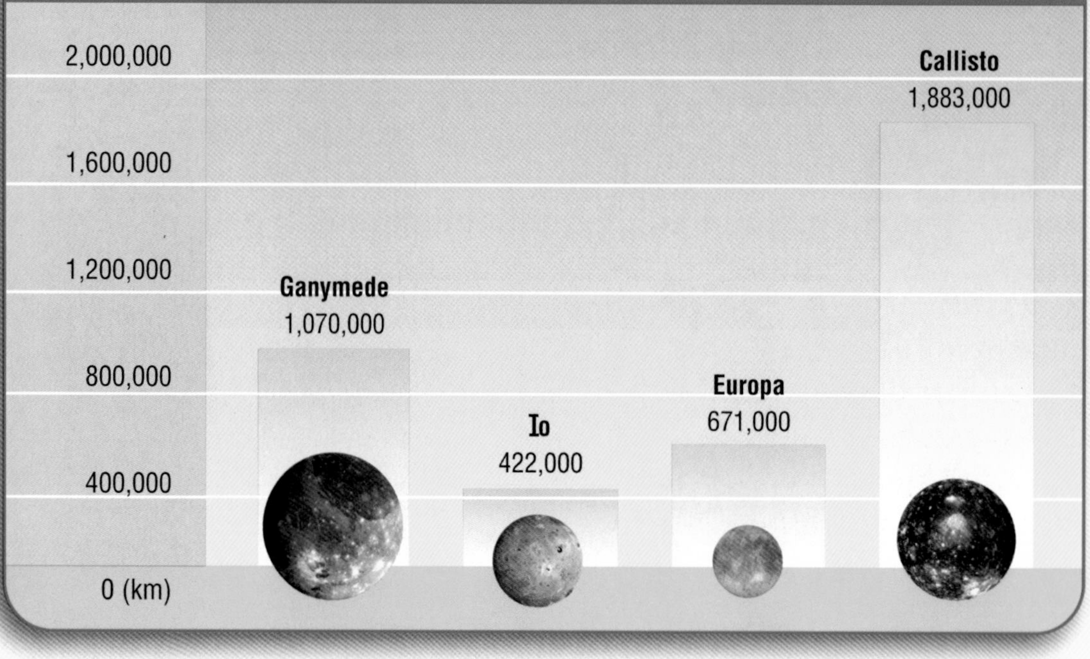

2,000,000

Callisto
1,883,000

1,600,000

1,200,000

Ganymede
1,070,000

800,000

Europa
671,000

Io
422,000

400,000

0 (km)

Practice the Skill

Answer the following questions to interpret the data that have been collected about Io, Europa, Ganymede, and Callisto.

1. Which moon is farthest from Jupiter?

2. Which moon is closest to Jupiter?

3. Find the difference between Io's average distance and Callisto's average distance from Jupiter.

4. List the four large moons in order from most distant to closest to Jupiter.

Check It Out

Mass and distance affect the force of gravity. The more massive two objects are and the closer they are, the greater the pull of gravity. Look at the graph on page 26. Which of the two largest Galilean satellites—Ganymede or Callisto—is most affected by Jupiter's gravity?

Focus On

》》》

**Ellen Ochoa:
NASA Astronaut**

As an astronaut and engineer, Ellen Ochoa has already been on several space flights. Ochoa studies robotics. In the lab, she interprets data from robotics research for use in the space station. On her missions into space, Ochoa uses robotic arms to retrieve satellites and transfer equipment to the International Space Station.

How a Rocket Works

It's too dangerous to stand near a rocket when it blasts off.
But you can use a balloon and string to make a model of how
a rocket works. Try this activity to build your own model.

Materials

- ✔ String
- ✔ Scissors
- ✔ Plastic straw
- ✔ Long balloon
- ✔ Meterstick
- ✔ Clothespin
- ✔ Tape
- ✔ Safety goggles

SAFETY TIP: Always wear your safety goggles when you work with balloons.

Explore

(Work with a partner.)

1 Cut a piece of string about 5 meters (16 feet) long.

2 Thread one end of the string through a straw. *(See photograph A.)*

3 Tie one end of the string to a chair. Tie the other end to another chair that is about 4 meters (13 feet) away.

A

B

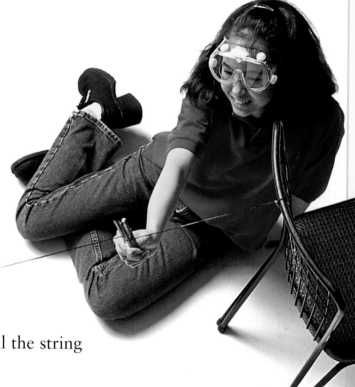

4 Move the chairs apart until the string is tight and level.

5 Blow up the balloon and clip the clothespin to the end so air cannot escape.

6 Tape the balloon to the middle of the straw. (*See photograph B.*)

7 Move the straw with the balloon close to a chair. Make sure the end with the clothespin is closest to the chair.

8 Remove the clothespin.

9 Measure how far the balloon moves. Record the distance.

10 Repeat steps 5 to 9 four times.

Think

What do you think causes the balloon to move forward? What is used, instead of air, in a real rocket launch?

Science Notebook

SPACE TRIVIA

- A message describing Earth was sent into space in 1974. The radio telescope message will take more than 20,000 years to reach its destination in the Milky Way Galaxy.

- The tallest known volcano in our solar system is on Mars. Olympus Mons rises as high as three Mount Everests—the highest mountain on Earth.

- In 1995 Valerie Ambroise, age 12, won an essay contest to name the Mars *Pathfinder* rover. She wrote about Sojourner Truth, an African-American woman born into slavery around 1797 and freed in 1827. After winning her freedom, Truth spent the rest of her life speaking against slavery and supporting women's rights. The *Pathfinder* rover was named Sojourner in her honor.

Pathfinder rover

PLACES TO CONTACT

NASA Headquarters
Washington, D.C. 20546

Amazing Space: Lessons from the Hubble Space Telescope
Space Telescope Science Institute
3700 San Martin Dr.
Baltimore, MD 21218
amazing-space.stsci.edu

BOOKS TO READ

Dyson, Marianne J. *Space Station Science: Life in Free Fall*. Scholastic, 1999. This book answers questions about living in a space station.

Ride, Sally, and Tam O'Shaughnessy. *The Mystery of Mars*. Crown Publishing, 1999. This is a great book for anyone who is interested in learning more about the Red Planet.

WEBSITES TO VISIT

NASA Kids: *kids.msfc.nasa.gov*

NASA Space Science for Kids: *spacekids.hq.nasa.gov*

To track the current location of the space station: *spaceflight.nasa.gov/realdata/tracking/index.html*

Glossary

asteroid *(AS-tuh-roid)* – one of the many small bodies orbiting the sun, mostly in the region between Mars and Jupiter

comet *(KOM-it)* – a large chunk of ice, dust, and gas that travels around the sun in a long path

communications satellite *(kuh-mune-i-KAY-shunz SAT-ul-ite)* – an orbiting artificial Earth satellite that relays radio, television, and other signals between ground stations thousands of miles apart

constellation *(kahn-stuh-LAY-shun)* – a group of stars that seem to make a pattern in the sky

galaxy *(GAL-uk-see)* – a very large group of stars and clouds of gas and dust that are fairly close together in space

gravity – the pull of an object on another object

International Space Station *(in-ter-NASH-nul SPASE STAY-shun)* – a permanent city in space—built through a cooperative effort between 16 nations—where an international crew can live and work

interpret data *(in-TER-prit DAY-tuh)* – explain information

meteor *(MEE-tee-ur)* – a small body that causes a fiery streak of light in the sky as it passes through Earth's atmosphere and burns up

meteorite *(MEE-tee-uh-rite)* – a meteor that has fallen to the surface of a planet or moon

meteoroid *(MEE-tee-uh-roid)* – a piece of rock or dust in space. When a meteoroid enters Earth's atmosphere, it becomes a meteor or meteorite.

orbit – a path around a heavenly body

physics – science that deals with matter and energy

satellite *(SAT-ul-ite)* – a smaller body that revolves around a larger body such as a planet

solar system *(SOH-lur SIS-tum)* – the collection of planets, moons, asteroids, and comets that orbit the sun

virtual reality *(VURCH-oo-uhl ree-AL-uh-tee)* – a three-dimensional environment that is created by a computer but that seems real to the user

weather satellite *(WETH-ur SAT-ul-ite)* – an orbiting object in space that monitors weather conditions on Earth

Index